Table of Contents

Cooking Professional, **page 7**

Outdoor Adventurer, **page 18**

Medical Professional, **page 24**

Yoga Enthusiast, **page 14**

Love to Dress for Work & Play is published by DRG, 306 East Parr Road, Berne, IN 46711. Printed in USA. Copyright © 2011 DRG. All rights reserved. This publication may not be reproduced in part or in whole without written permission from the publisher.

RETAIL STORES: If you would like to carry this pattern book or any other DRG publications, visit DRGwholesale.com

Every effort has been made to ensure that the instructions in this pattern book are complete and accurate. We cannot, however, take responsibility for human error, typographical mistakes or variations in individual work. Please visit ClotildeCustomerCare.com to check for pattern updates.

HOUSE of WHITE BIRCHES
PUBLISHERS SINCE 1947

ISBN: 978-1-59217-359-4

1 2 3 4 5 6 7 8 9

House of White Birches, Berne, Indiana 46711   Clotilde.com

Love to Dress for Work & Play

It seemed a good idea to mix outfits suitable for both work and play within the pages of my next 18-inch doll clothes book and I decided I wanted to work with themes. I realized after completing the designs that I could relate each set with a particular person in my life.

My youngest daughter, Kimberly, is an ER nurse and I have made a few sets of scrubs over the past couple of years. The Medical Professional designs are dedicated to her and folks just like her that work to take such good care of us all when we are not at our best. The Cooking Professional designs are a direct result of my eldest daughter Jocelyn's love of cooking and baking. The Outdoor Explorer designs were inspired by a close family friend named Kristi, who loves all things outdoors and enjoys hiking, kayaking and riding her bicycle. Finally, while no expert in yoga, I admire the dedication and cool yoga outfits of the folks that surround me at the gym. Someday I will try a yoga class but, for now, I'll design and sew cool yoga clothes for dolls and work out on the treadmill.

Fat quarters remain my first fabric choice for the doll clothes in my books. They really do simplify the process of choosing the fabric. There is no need to carry heavy bolts of fabric around the store, no decisions as to how much fabric to purchase and no waiting in line to have the fabric cut! Simply choose your favorite print(s), which are ever so neatly folded into perfect little squares, and head to the cash register!

My hope is that you have as much fun creating clothes for your 18-inch doll as I did in designing and selecting the fabrics for the designs in this book.

Sew far sew good,

Meet the Designer

Lorine Mason is an author, licensed artist, project designer and editor of the Sewing Savvy e-letter. Her work has been featured in print, on the Web and television. She works with a variety of art mediums, combining them with her enthusiasm for all things fabric. She strives to create items others will be inspired to re-create, hopefully adding their own personal touches. Her creative career started in retail, weaving its way through management and education positions along the way. This experience, along with a goal to stay on top of trends in color and style, gives her current work the edge that manufacturers, publishers and editors have come to expect. She shares her life with her husband, Bill, and daughters Jocelyn and Kimberly in Virginia.

General Instructions

The Fit Factor

Using a generic term such as 18-inch dolls can be misleading since dolls, not unlike people, will not have the same measurements even if their height might be similar. A few minutes spent measuring your doll is a good idea. When drafting the patterns for this book, I used 11 inches for the chest and waist measurements, and 12 inches for the hip measurement.

The clothing designs featured in this book were fitted using the Springfield Collection® and the American Girl® 18-inch dolls. I found the American Girl dolls were slightly larger, therefore I took this into account when drafting the patterns. I know there are many other varieties of dolls for which you might be inclined to use these patterns, therefore take a moment and measure your dolls before proceeding, being sure to make any necessary pattern adjustments before cutting out your pattern pieces.

Fabric Selection

All of the outfits and accessories in this book were made using fat quarters. Available in colorful patterns and packaging, fat quarters are the "candy" in the fabric store and are a wonderful way to coordinate fabrics. Generally available in 18 x 22-inch cuts, fat quarters are equivalent to standard 9 x 45-inch quarter yards, and any cotton fabric is suitable for these patterns.

Basic Sewing Supplies & Equipment
- Sewing machine and matching thread
- Scissors of various sizes, including pinking shears
- Rotary cutter(s), mats and straightedges
- Pattern-tracing paper or cloth
- Pressing tools such as sleeve rolls and June Tailor boards
- Pressing equipment, including ironing board and iron; press cloths
- Straight pins and pincushion
- Measuring tools
- Marking pens (either air- or water-soluble) or tailor's chalk
- Seam sealant
- Hand-sewing needles and thimble
- Point turners

Optional Supplies
- ¼-inch-wide double-sided basting tape
- Velcro Fusion® fastener strips
- Bias tape maker
- Tube-turning tool
- Mini iron
- Serger

Construction & Application Techniques

Bobbins

Fill multiple bobbins ahead of time with neutral colors of thread. A cream-colored thread was used for many of the garments in this book. Change only the top color of thread to either match or contrast with garment colors.

Basting

Basting is a way to hold fabric pieces in place without using pins. It is especially useful in tight places or on small projects. Basting can be done by hand or machine using a longer-than-normal stitch length to sew where indicated. Remove basting stitches after garment is permanently sewn.

Backstitching

Backstitching at least ¼ inch at the beginning and end of each seam to secure stitching. This ensures handling does not undo your seams.

Finishing Raw Edges

Every exposed seam should be finished for longer wear and cleaner construction. Finish raw edges with zigzag or overcast stitches or by using a serger. This can be done to each garment piece prior to sewing the garment or during construction.

Gathering

1. Make two rows of longer-than-normal stitches on either side of the seam line, leaving long thread tails at either end (Figure 1).

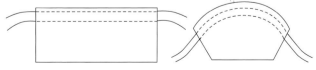

Figure 1

House of White Birches, Berne, Indiana 46711   Clotilde.com

2. With right sides together, pin gathered section to appropriate garment section at each end and at the center (Figure 2).

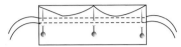

Figure 2

3. Pull bobbin threads at one end to gather. When half of gathered section fits straight-edge length, secure bobbin threads by twisting around pin (Figure 3). Repeat for second half of section. Pin securely along seam line, adjusting gathers evenly.

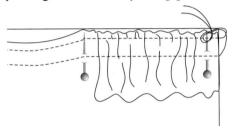

Figure 3

4. Stitch at seam line with gathered section on top (Figure 4). Keep gathers even so folds of fabric do not form while stitching.

Figure 4

5. Remove gathering stitches after sewing seam.

Topstitching

Topstitching provides a decorative touch, while strengthening seams and edges. Because of the ¼-inch seams used in these projects, we suggest topstitching open seams from the wrong side. Stitch approximately ⅛ inch from the seam line or from the finished edge.

Bias-Tape Bound Edges

1. Leaving bias tape folded, sandwich raw edges of garment between bias tape so the fabric raw edge meets the center fold of the bias tape (Figure 5).

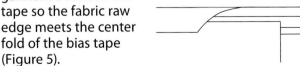

Figure 5

2. Edgestitch bias tape to secure (Figure 6). ***Note:*** *Purchased bias tape has one side wider than the other. Be sure to edgestitch with shorter side up when using purchased bias tape.*

Figure 6

Bias-Tape Hems & Casings

1. Press center fold of bias tape flat, leaving edges folded (Figure 7).

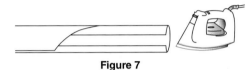

Figure 7

2. Pin raw edge of bias tape along fabric raw edge and stitch in edge fold (Figure 8).

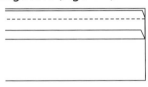

Figure 8

3. Press bias tape to wrong side and stitch along edge fold (Figure 9).

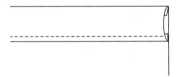

Figure 9

Collars

1. Mark collar neckline center. Pin and stitch collar sections right sides together using a ¼-inch seam allowance. Do not stitch neckline seam (Figure 10).

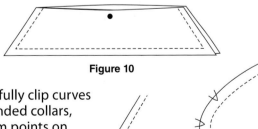

Figure 10

2. Carefully clip curves on rounded collars, and trim points on pointed collars (Figure 11). Turn, using point turner in corners. Press.

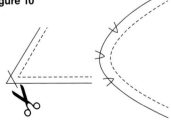

Figure 11

3. Pin, and then baste collar to garment neckline, matching collar center to garment center back (Figure 12).

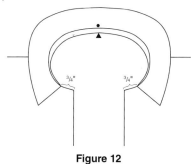

Figure 12

4. Collar will be stitched in place when facing is applied.

Facings

1. Stitch facings together at center back seam (Figure 13). Press seam open.

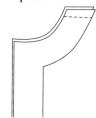

Figure 13

2. Apply bias tape to outside edges (Figure 14).
Note: Refer to general instructions on bias-tape application for bound edges.

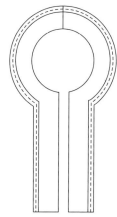

Figure 14

3. Pin facing to garment neckline and front edges, right sides together. Stitch using ¼-inch seam allowance (Figure 15).

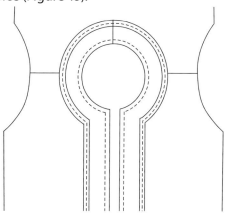

Figure 15

4. Clip curves and trim corners (Figure 16). Turn to right side and press.

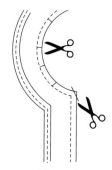

Figure 16

5. Edgestitch facing through all layers using coordinating thread (Figure 17).

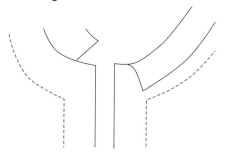

Figure 17

Sleeves

1. Stitch two rows of gathering stitches at sleeve cap (Figure 18). *Note: Refer to general instructions on gathering (page 3).*

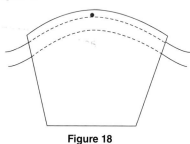

Figure 18

2. With right sides together, pin sleeve cap center to garment shoulder seam and edges of sleeve to garment sides (Figure 19). Gather sleeve cap to fit garment armhole and pin securely.

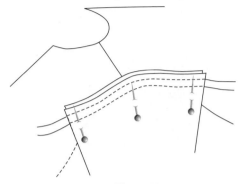

Figure 19

3. Stitch using a ¼-inch seam allowance. Press seam allowance toward sleeve (Figure 20).

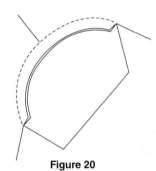

Figure 20

4. With right sides together, match armhole seams and pin underarm seam. Stitch using a ¼-inch seam allowance (Figure 21).

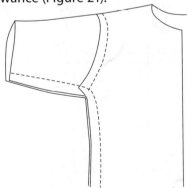

Figure 21

Single Hem

1. Press at least ¼ inch to wrong side of garment (Figure 22).

Figure 22

2. Measuring from the folded edge just made, press the hem width indicated in individual instructions to garment wrong side. (Figure 23).

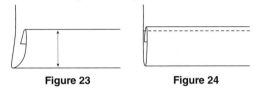

Figure 23   **Figure 24**

3. Edgestitch close to second fold (Figure 24).

4. If desired, use a contrasting thread to add a simple decorative finish to hems.

Double-Turned ¼-Inch Hem

1. Press ¼ inch to wrong side of section (Figure 25).

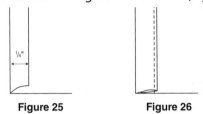

Figure 25   **Figure 26**

2. Turn and press again ¼ inch to wrong side. Edgestitch close to second fold (Figure 26).

Fastener Application

1. Try finished garment on doll to determine where fasteners should be positioned to fit doll's girth.

2. Mark position with pin, lapping garment right side over left (Figure 27).

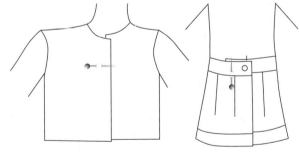

Figure 27

3. Apply ½-inch pieces of fusible hook-and-loop tape to right and left sides of garment where marked. Add decorative closures to right side of garment over hook-and-loop tape.

Option: If using snaps, sew male side of snap to right side, and female side of snap to left side of garment (Figure 28). ❖

Figure 28

Cooking Professional

What's cooking? In this cute chef attire it won't matter—what's brewing here is hours of fun!

Chef's Coat

Materials
- 2 coordinating fat quarters (A, B)
- 4 x 18-inch piece lightweight fusible interfacing
- 2 inches ¾-inch-wide fusible hook & loop tape
- 1 package coordinating bias tape
- 8 (½-inch) buttons
- Basic sewing supplies and equipment

Cutting
Use pattern templates C4–C6, M3, O8 (pages 29, 30, 31, 39 and 45). Transfer all pattern markings to fabric.

From fabric A:
- Cut two Chef's Coat Fronts (C4), reversing one.
- Cut one Chef's Coat Back (C5).
- Cut two Sleeves (M3).
- Cut one Chef's Coat Collar (C6).

From fabric B:
- Cut two Facings (O8).
- Cut one Chef's Coat Collar (C6).

From interfacing:
- Cut two Facings (O8).
- Cut one Chef's Coat Collar (C6).

Assembly
Stitch right sides together using a ¼-inch seam allowance unless otherwise specified. Refer to General Instructions (page 3) for finishing all seams and for the following construction techniques: Single Hem, Double-Turned ¼-Inch Hem, Sleeves, Bias-Tape Bound Edges, Facings, Collars, Fastener Application and Topstitching.

1. Following manufacturer's instructions, fuse interfacing to the wrong side of one Collar (C6) and both Facing pieces (08).

2. Stitch Fronts (C4) and Back (C5) together at shoulder seams.

3. Construct and baste Collar (C6) to the neckline, matching placement marks.

4. Construct and stitch Facings to the Chef's Coat, matching notches and shoulder seams.

5. Topstitch the Facing to the back of the jacket between the shoulder seams.

6. Stitch a Double-Turned ¼-Inch Hem along the bottom edge of the Sleeves.

7. Stitch Sleeves to Chef's Coat, matching notches.

8. Stitch Fronts to Back with right sides together at side seams and along underarm seams.

9. Stitch a Single Hem to bottom edge of the Chef's Coat.

10. Apply three fusible hook-and-loop tape fasteners to the Chef's Coat Front.

11. Sew eight buttons to the right front of the Chef's Coat at placement marks and as shown in Figure 1.

Figure 1

Chef's Pants

Materials
- 1 fat quarter
- 11 inches ¼-inch elastic
- Basic sewing supplies and equipment

Cutting
Use pattern template S6 (page 48). Transfer all pattern markings to fabric.

From fabric:
- Cut four Pants (S6), reversing two.

Assembly
Stitch right sides together using a ¼-inch seam allowance unless otherwise specified. Refer to General Instructions (page 3) for finishing all seams and for the following construction techniques: Double-Turned ¼-Inch Hem and Topstitching.

1. Stitch Pant Fronts and Backs (S6) together along side seams, matching notches (Figure 2). Press seams to one side and Topstitch in place.

Figure 2

2. Stitch center front Pants seam, referring to Figure 3. Press seam to one side and Topstitch in place.

Figure 3

3. Create a waistline elastic casing by pressing on the first fold line to the wrong side. Press again on the second fold line to the wrong side. Stitch close to the first fold line (Figure 4).

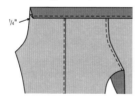

Figure 4

4. Thread elastic through casing, pinning ends of elastic even with back seam. Stitch to secure (Figure 5).

Figure 5

5. Stitch a Double-Turned ¼-Inch Hem along bottom edge of each of the Pant legs.

6. Stitch Pants center back seam. Press to one side and Topstitch in place.

7. Sew inner leg seams to complete Pants.

Chef's Apron & Coordinating Pants

Materials
- 2 coordinating fat quarters (A, B)
- 1 package ¼-inch double-fold contrasting bias tape
- Contrasting general-purpose thread
- Basic sewing supplies and equipment

Cutting
Use pattern templates C2 and C3 (page 29). Transfer all pattern markings to fabric.

From fabric A:
- Cut one Chef's Apron (C2).
- Cut one Chef's Apron Pocket (C3).

From fabric B:
- Cut one Chef's Apron Pocket (C3).

From bias tape:
- Cut two 20-inch pieces.

Assembly
Stitch right sides together using a ¼-inch seam allowance unless otherwise specified. Refer to General Instructions (page 3) for finishing all seams and for Double-Turned ¼-Inch Hem and Topstitching.

Chef's Apron

1. With right sides together, stitch Pocket pieces (C3) together along the top and bottom edges. Turn right side out and press.

2. Topstitch ⅛ inch from the top edge.

3. Pin Pocket to the Apron front at position marked on the pattern.

4. Topstitch the bottom edge of Pocket to Apron, sewing two rows of stitching ⅛ inch apart using contrasting, general-purpose thread.

5. Topstitch along marked stitching lines to divide Pocket into thirds (Figure 6).

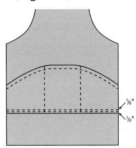

Figure 6

6. Stitch Double-Turned ¼-Inch Hems at the top, sides and bottom edges of Apron. Topstitch two rows ⅛ inch apart using contrasting, general-purpose thread.

7. Bind Apron underarm edges with 20-inch pieces of ¼-inch contrasting bias tape, extending bias tape 8 inches beyond neck and side ends as shown in Figure 7.

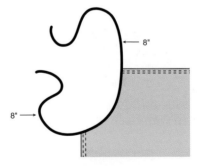

Figure 7

Coordinating Pants

The Coordinating Pants featured in the photograph are created using the pattern pieces and instructions from Chef's Pants on page 8.

Chef's Cap

Materials
- 2 coordinating fat quarters (A, B)
- 4 x 18-inch lightweight fusible interfacing
- 1½ inches ¾-inch-wide fusible hook-and-loop tape
- Basic sewing supplies and equipment

Cutting
Use pattern template C1 (page 32). Transfer all pattern markings to fabric.

From fabric A:
- Cut one Chef's Cap (C1).

From fabric B:
- Cut one 3 x 14-inch rectangle for Cap band.
- Cut one 1 x 6-inch bias strip referring to Making Bias Tape.

From interfacing:
- Cut one 3 x 14-inch rectangle for Cap band.

Making Bias Tape
Make your own bias tape to add a distinctive flair to any project. Instructions are for ¼-inch finished-size bias tape.

1. Fold fabric diagonally so crosswise grain straight edge is parallel to selvage or lengthwise grain. Cut fabric along this fold line to mark the true bias (Figure 1).

Figure 1

2. Using a clear ruler, mark successive bias lines 1 inch wide. Carefully cut along lines. Handle edges carefully to avoid stretching (Figure 2).

Figure 2

3. Sew short ends of strips together as shown in Figure 3.

Figure 3

4. Fold strip in half lengthwise, wrong sides together. Press.

5. Open out with wrong side up. Fold each edge to center fold and press. Fold in half again and press.

Assembly

Stitch right sides together using a ¼-inch seam allowance unless otherwise specified. Refer to General Instructions (page 3) for finishing all seams.

1. Stitch on slit stitching line to reinforce using a short stitch length.

2. Unfold bias tape and pin to right side of slit opening, matching first bias tape fold line to slit stitching line and stitch (Figure 8).

Figure 8

3. Press bias to wrong side, covering seam line, and pin.

4. Edgestitch bias tape on right side, catching bias-tape edge on wrong side in seam. Trim bias tape even with Cap edges.

5. Sew two rows of gathering stitches ⅛ and ¼ inch from raw edge of Chef's Cap.

6. Follow manufacturer's instructions to fuse interfacing to wrong side of Cap band.

7. Fold band in half lengthwise, right sides together, and stitch short ends. Turn right side out; press and baste raw edges together.

8. Apply 1½ inches of fusible hook-and-loop tape to opposite sides of band ends (Figure 9).

Figure 9

9. Pin crown to band, matching bound slit edges to band ends. Pull, gathering threads and evenly dispersing Cap gathers to fit band (Figure 10).

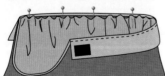

Figure 10

10. Pin to hold and stitch. Remove any basting or gathering stitches and press seam toward crown.

Chef's Shirt

Materials
- 1 plain white fat quarter
- 1 package white ¼-inch-wide double-fold bias tape
- 1½ inches ¾-inch-wide heat-activated fusible hook-and-loop tape
- Basic sewing supplies and equipment

Cutting
Use pattern templates C7–C9 (pages 33 and 34). Transfer all pattern markings to fabric.

From fat quarter:
- Cut one Chef's Shirt Back (C7) on fold.
- Cut two Chef's Shirt Front (C8), reverse one.
- Cut two Chef's Sleeves (C9), reverse one.

From ¾-inch-wide heat-activated fusible hook-and-loop tape:
- Cut three ½ x ¾-inch fasteners.

Assembly
Stitch right sides together using a ¼-inch seam allowance unless otherwise specified. Refer to General Instructions (page 3) for finishing all seams and for the following construction techniques: Sleeves, Topstitching, Bias-Tape Bound Edges, Double-Turned ¼-Inch Hem and Fastener Application.

1. Sew Chef's Shirt Back (C7) and Chef's Shirt Front (C8) together at shoulder seams.

2. Bind neckline edge.

3. Stitch a Double-Turned ¼-Inch Hem on sleeve bottom edges, turning under ⅛ inch instead of ¼ inch.

4. Stitch Sleeves to shirt.

5. Stitch a Double-Turned ¼-Inch Hem on both center back edges, turning under ⅛ inch instead of ¼ inch.

6. Stitch a Double-Turned ¼-Inch Hem around bottom edge of shirt, turning under ⅛ inch instead of ¼ inch.

7. Apply three fusible hook-and-loop fasteners to shirt back. ❖

Yoga Enthusiast

All this and a yoga mat too! Besides, even dolly is more fun to be with after a yoga session. Sew these quick and easy projects and watch the good times begin.

Yoga Top

Materials
- 1 fat quarter
- 1 package ¼-inch-wide double-fold bias tape
- 1 (1½ x 2-inch) iron-on appliqué
- 1 inch ¾-inch-wide fusible hook-and-loop tape
- Basic sewing supplies and equipment

Cutting
Use pattern templates Y1–Y4 (pages 35, 36 and 37). Transfer all pattern markings to fabric.

From fabric:
- Cut one Yoga Top Front (Y1).
- Cut two Yoga Top Back and Facing pieces (Y2), reversing one.
- Cut one Yoga Top Front Facing (Y4).
- Cut two Yoga Sleeves (Y3).

Assembly
Stitch right sides together using a ¼-inch seam allowance unless otherwise specified. Refer to General Instructions (page 3) for finishing all seams and for the following construction techniques: Bias-Tape Bound Edges, Sleeves, Fastener Application, Topstitching and Facings.

1. Stitch Yoga Top Front (Y1) and Backs (Y2) together at shoulder seams.

2. Stitch Yoga Top Front Facing (Y4) to Back Facings at shoulder seams (Figure 1). Press seam open. Bind outer edge of Facing with bias tape.

Figure 1

3. Fold Facing to wrong side along fold line, matching neckline edges and side seams to Yoga Top (Figure 2). Pin and stitch; clip curves and trim corners.

Figure 2

4. Turn right side out and press. Tack Facing to shoulder at seam.

5. Bind bottom edges of Yoga Sleeves (Y3) with bias tape.

6. Stitch Sleeves to Yoga Top.

7. Stitch underarm seams and side seams.

8. Bind bottom edge of Yoga Top with bias tape, turning under short edges of bias tape at each end.

9. Apply three fusible hook-and-loop fasteners to back of Yoga Top.

10. Following manufacturer's instructions, center and fuse an iron-on appliqué to the front of the Top.

Yoga Pants

Materials
- 2 coordinating fat quarters (A, B)
- 4-inch piece of ½-inch elastic
- Contrasting general-purpose thread
- Basic sewing supplies and equipment

Cutting
Use pattern templates Y5–Y8 (pages 31, 36 and 38). Transfer all pattern markings to fabric.

From fabric A:
• Cut two each of Yoga Pant Front A (Y5), Yoga Pant Front B (Y6) and Yoga Pant Back (Y7).

From fabric B:
• Cut one Yoga Pant Waistband (Y8).

Assembly

Stitch right sides together using a ¼-inch seam unless otherwise specified. Refer to General Instructions (page 3) for finishing all seams and for the following construction techniques: Double-Turned ¼-Inch Hem, Single-Fold Hem and Topstitching.

1. Stitch Yoga Pant Front A and B right sides together from waist to X using a ½-inch seam allowance (Figure 3). Press seam open.

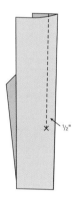

Figure 3

2. Topstitch from waist to bottom edge using contrasting general-purpose thread on both sides of seam.

3. Stitch Pant Fronts and Backs (Y7) together along side seams, matching notches (Figure 4). Press seams to one side and Topstitch in place.

Figure 4

4. Stitch center Front and Back seams (Figure 5). Press seams to one side and Topstitch.

Figure 5

5. Press fabric of Waistband toward wrong side on first fold line, then on casing fold line.

6. With right sides together, stitch Waistband together along short ends. Press seams open and Topstitch.

7. With right sides together, pin Waistband to Yoga Pants waist, matching center back seams, and stitch. Press seams toward Waistband and Topstitch through all layers of fabric.

8. To create elastic casing, press ¼ inch to wrong side along top of the Waistband, then press again to wrong side along casing line. Pin along first fold line.

9. Edgestitch through all layers between marks along first fold, forming a casing at the back of the Waistband (Figure 6).

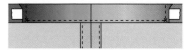

Figure 6

10. Insert the elastic, pinning each end, stretching elastic to fit. Edgestitch through all layers to secure, again referring to Figure 6.

11. Complete edgestitching along first fold line and casing fold line to finish Waistband.

12. Stitch a Double-Turned ¼-Inch Hem along the bottom edge of the Pant legs.

13. Stitch inner leg seam, matching notches and center front and back seams to complete.

Yoga Carryall & Mat

Materials

- 1 fat quarter
- 14 inches cotton cording
- 1 plastic drawstring spring lock
- 1 sheet 11 x 17-inch craft foam sheet
- Basic sewing supplies and equipment

Cutting

Transfer all pattern markings to fabric.

From fabric:

- Cut one 5 x 18-inch rectangle.

Assembly

Stitch right sides together using a ¼-inch seam allowance unless otherwise specified. Refer to General Instructions (page 3) for finishing all seams.

Mat Carryall

1. Fold the 5 x 18-inch rectangle right sides together forming a 5 x 9-inch rectangle.

2. Stitch long sides together starting at fold and ending 2 inches from top edge (Figure 7). Press seams open, continuing to press past the end of the seam to top of bag.

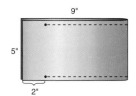

Figure 7

3. Topstitch along each side of the fold from top edge to ¼ inch past seam line along each side (Figure 8).

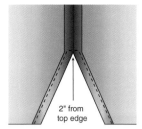

2" from top edge

Figure 8

4. Fold top of bag ¼ inch and then ½ inch to wrong side. Edgestitch along last fold to form a casing on top edges of both front and back sections (Figure 9).

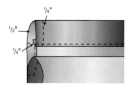

Figure 9

5. Thread cording through casing. Attach spring clip to cord ends. Tie cord ends together.

Yoga Mat

1. Cut one 6½ x 16-inch rectangle from craft foam in the color of your choice

2. Roll mat and place in carryall. ❖

Outdoor Adventurer

Lions and tigers and bears … maybe not, but proper dressing
for the great outdoors makes any trip more exciting.

Vest
Materials
- 2 coordinating fat quarters (A, B)
- One ½-inch plastic prong closure
- 7 mini buttons
- Hook-and-loop tape fasteners
- Basic sewing supplies and equipment

Cutting
Use pattern templates O4, O5 and M5 (pages 39, 44 and 45). Transfer all pattern markings to fabric.

From fabric A:
- Cut two Vest Fronts (O4), reversing one.
- Cut one Vest Back (O5).
- Cut two Large Pockets (M5).
- Cut one 2½ x 15-inch strip for hemline band.
- Cut one 2 x 15-inch strip for belt.
- Cut two 1 x 18-inch bias-tape strips referring to Making Bias Tape on page 11.

From fabric B:
- Cut two Vest Fronts (O4), reversing one, for lining.
- Cut one Vest Back (O5) for lining.

Assembly
Stitch right sides together using a ¼-inch seam allowance unless otherwise specified. Refer to General Instructions (page 3) for finishing all seams and for the following construction techniques: Bias-Tape Bound Edges, Fastener Application, Double-Turned ¼-Inch Hem and Topstitching.

1. Stitch A Vest Fronts (O4) to Vest Back (O5) at shoulder seams. Repeat with B Fronts and Back.

2. With A and B Vest bodies right sides together, matching shoulder seams and edges of armholes, stitch around armholes (Figure 1). Clip curves close to seam. Turn right side out and press seam open at side seam edges.

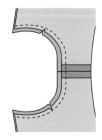

Figure 1

3. Match underarm seams and A and B sides to A and B sides, pin right sides together.

4. Sew side seams, starting at bottom edge of B and finishing at bottom edge of A Vest Front. Repeat for opposite side seam. Press seams open and turn right side out.

5. Baste raw edges of Vest and lining wrong sides together.

6. Fold and stitch the belt right sides together lengthwise. Turn right side out and press. Topstitch down either side of the belt.

7. Center and pin belt at placement markings on Vest Back and pin (Figure 2).

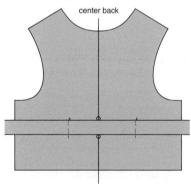

Figure 2

8. Press open center fold of one piece of bias tape and center over the belt along the center back, matching the top and bottom edges of the Vest (Figure 3).

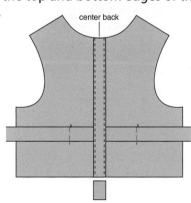

Figure 3

9. Topstitch down either side of the bias tape. Trim excess bias tape even with the bottom edge of the Vest, again referring to Figure 3.

10. Press hemline band in half lengthwise with right sides together. Open and press ¼ inch to wrong side along one long side.

11. Stitch un-pressed band edge bottom edge of Vest right sides together. Turn to lining side of Vest, matching pressed edge to seam line, and pin. Topstitch along seam line at the top and bottom edge of the band.

12. Turn under raw edge of one end of remaining bias-tape strip ¼ inch to wrong side. Pin binding over raw edges of Vest neckline and Front. Trim if necessary and turn under raw edge at the opposite end ¼ inch. Topstitch through all layers.

13. Slide prong closure onto the belt; adjust to fit doll. Turn under raw edges and Topstitch to secure closures onto belt (Figure 4).

Figure 4

14. Make Double-Turned ¼-Inch Hems on top of Pockets (M5). Then, press side and bottom seam allowances toward wrong side. Center and stitch one mini button on top hem of each Large Pocket. Stitch Pockets to Vest Fronts at placement markings.

15. Stitch five mini buttons evenly spaced along bias binding on right front of Vest.

16. Apply hook-and-loop tape fasteners to Vest.

Shorts

Materials
- 1 fat quarter
- 11-inch piece of ½-inch elastic
- Basic sewing supplies and equipment

Cutting
Use pattern templates O1, M5 and S5 (pages 40, 45 and 46). Transfer all pattern markings to fabric.

From fabric:
- Cut four Shorts (O1), reversing two.
- Cut two Large Pockets (M5).
- Cut two Large Pocket Flaps (S5).

Assembly

Stitch right sides together using a ¼-inch seam allowance unless otherwise specified. Refer to General Instructions (page 3) for finishing all seams and Topstitching.

1. Stitch Shorts fronts and backs along side seams (Figure 5). Press seams toward front. Topstitch in place.

Figure 5

2. Stitch center front seam (Figure 6). Press seam to one side and Topstitch in place.

Figure 6

3. Create a waistline elastic casing by pressing on the first fold line to the wrong side. Press again on the second fold line to the wrong side. Stitch close to the first fold line (Figure 7).

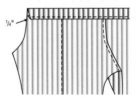

Figure 7

4. Thread elastic through casing, pinning ends of elastic even with back seam. Stitch to secure (Figure 8).

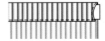

Figure 8

5. Press along first fold line to wrong side of leg edges. Then, press along second fold line to wrong side referring to Figure 9.

Figure 9

6. Press along third fold line to right side of leg edges to create cuff (Figure 10). Topstitch top and bottom edge of cuff, again referring to Figure 10.

Figure 10

7. Make Double-Turned ¼-Inch Hems on top of Large Pocket (M5). Then, press side and bottom seam allowances toward wrong side.

8. Match squares on Large Pocket to squares on Shorts and Topstitch sides and bottoms of all pockets.

9. Fold pocket flap in half wrong sides together and stitch short sides together. Turn right side out and press.

10. Match circles on Large Pocket Flap to circles on Shorts and stitch between circles through Flap and Shorts. Press Flap down and Topstitch (Figure 11).

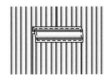

Figure 11

11. Repeat steps 7–10 for second Pocket.

12. Stitch Shorts center back seam. Press to one side and Topstitch in place.

13. Sew inner leg seams to complete.

Button-Down Shirt

Materials
- 1 fat quarter
- 4 x 12-inch lightweight fusible interfacing
- 1 package ¼-inch-wide double-fold bias tape
- 7 mini buttons
- Basic sewing supplies and equipment

Cutting
Use pattern templates O6–O9 and M3 (pages 39, 41, 43 and 45). Transfer all pattern markings to fabric.

From fabric:
- Cut two Shirt Fronts (O6), reversing one.
- Cut one Shirt Back (O7).
- Cut two Sleeves (M3).
- Cut two Collars (O9).
- Cut two Facings (O8).

From interfacing:
- Cut two Facings (O8).

Assembly
Stitch right sides together using a ¼-inch seam allowance unless otherwise specified. Refer to General Instructions (page 3) for finishing all seams and for the following construction techniques: Sleeves, Double-Turned ¼-Inch Hem, Fastener Application, Topstitching, Facings and Collars.

1. Sew Shirt Fronts (O6) and Back (O7) together at shoulder seams, matching notches. Press seams toward front and Topstitch ⅛ inch away from seam.

2. Construct and baste Collar (O9) to shirt body.

3. Construct and stitch Facings (O8) to shirt body.

4. Stitch a Double-Turned ¼-Inch Hem to the bottom of each Sleeve.

5. Stitch sleeves to Shirt body, matching notches.

6. Sew underarm and sides of Shirt together. Press seams toward front of Shirt and Topstitch close to the seam line.

7. Stitch a Double-Turned ¼-Inch Hem at bottom edge of Shirt.

8. Stitch two rows of Topstitching on center front edges of Shirt.

9. Stitch seven mini buttons evenly spaced on right side of Button-Down Shirt Front.

10. Apply hook-and-loop fasteners to Shirt front opening.

Bucket Hat

Materials
- 2 coordinating fat quarters (A, B)
- ¼ yard lightweight fusible interfacing
- 12 inches ¼-inch-wide double-fold bias tape
- Basic sewing supplies and equipment

Cutting
Use pattern templates O2, O3 and M8 (pages 41, 42 and 44). Transfer all pattern markings to fabric.

From fabric A, B and interfacing:
- Cut one Brim (O2).
- Cut one Band (O3).
- Cut one Crown (M8).

Assembly
Stitch right sides together using a ¼-inch seam allowance unless otherwise specified. Refer to General Instructions (page 3) for Bias-Tape Bound Edges.

1. Following manufacturer's instructions, fuse interfacing to the wrong side of fabric A Brim (O2), Band (O3) and Crown (M8).

2. With right sides together, stitch each Brim (O2) together at short ends. Press seams open.

3. With right sides together, stitch each Band (O3) together at short ends. Press seams open.

4. Stitch the Brim pieces right sides together around outside edge (Figure 12). Clip curves close to stitching, turn right side out and press.

Figure 12

5. Stitch ⅛ inch from one edge of each Brim piece. Clip close to line of stitching.

6. With right sides together and matching fabrics, pin Bands to either side of Brim, matching back seams and stitch (Figure 13a). Press Band sections away from the Brim.

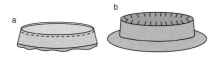

Figure 13

7. Baste together the Bands with a ⅛-inch seam. Clip close to the basting referring to Figure 13b.

8. Baste fabric A and B Crown pieces wrong sides together.

9. Matching raw edges, stitch the Crown to the Band with fabric A Band facing fabric A Crown (Figure 14).

Figure 14

10. Bind the seam with bias tape.

Backpack

Materials
- 2 coordinating fat quarters
- 12 inches cotton cording
- 24 inches ½-inch-wide cotton twill tape
- 1 plastic drawstring spring lock
- Basic sewing supplies and equipment

Cutting
Use pattern templates O10 and O11 (page 42). Transfer all pattern markings to fabric.

From fabric:
- Cut one Backpack (O10).
- Cut one Backpack Pocket (O11).
- Cut one 2 x 8-inch rectangle for drawstring casing.

From twill tape:
- Cut two 10-inch pieces for handles.
- Cut one 4-inch piece for Pocket trim.

Assembly
Stitch right sides together using a ¼-inch seam allowance unless otherwise specified.

1. Turn ¼ inch to right side along the top edge of Backpack Pocket (O11). Pin 4-inch piece of twill tape even with the fold and Topstitch along top and bottom edges for Pocket trim.

2. Turn bottom edge of Pocket ¼ inch to wrong side and press. Pin Pocket to front of Backpack at the position marked on the pattern.

3. Topstitch along bottom edge of Pocket. Topstitch on marked center stitching line (Figure 15).

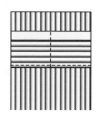

Figure 15

4. Pin one end of a 10-inch piece of twill tape to side seam at marked placement circles.

5. Pin the opposite end of the twill tape to second set of marked placement circles on same side of Backpack (Figure 16). Repeat for the opposite side.

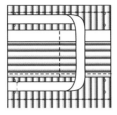

Figure 16

6. Fold the Backpack in half crosswise, right sides together, and stitch along each side. Turn right side out and press.

7. Turn short ends of drawstring casing ½ inch to wrong side and Topstitch.

8. Fold drawstring casing in half lengthwise and press. Open fold and press one raw edge ¼ inch to wrong side.

9. With right sides together, pin drawstring casing to top of Backpack with short hemmed edges butting together along left side of Backpack. Stitch along ¼-inch pressed line.

10. Press drawstring casing up and over Backpack top with pressed edge of drawstring casing slightly over seam. Hand- or machine-stitch in place to finish casing.

11. Thread cording through the casing. Insert ends of cording through spring lock and tie knots to prevent ends from slipping through the lock. ❖

Medical Professional

The diagnosis could be grim, but dolly will be delivering it in style in these medical professional outfits.

Lab Coat With Matching Scrub Cap

Materials
- 2 white-with-black fat quarters
- 10 black mini-plastic buttons
- Scrap lightweight fusible interfacing
- 1 package black ½-inch-wide single-fold bias tape
- 1¼ inches ¾-inch-wide fusible hook-and-loop tape
- Basic sewing supplies and equipment

Cutting
Use pattern templates M1–M7 (pages 32, 45, 46 and 47). Transfer all pattern markings to fabric.

From fat quarter:
- Cut two Lab Coat Fronts (M1), reversing one.
- Cut one Lab Coat Back (M2) on fold.
- Cut two Lab Coat Collar (M7) on fold.
- Cut two Lab Coat Facings (M6), reversing one.
- Cut two Sleeves (M3).
- Cut two Large Pockets (M5).
- Cut one Breast Pocket (M4).
- Cut one 2 x 9½-inch rectangle for belt.

From interfacing:
- Cut two Lab Coat Facings (M6), reversing one.
- Cut one Lab Coat Collar (M7).

Assembly
Stitch right sides together using a ¼-inch seam allowance unless otherwise specified. Refer to General Instructions (page 3) for finishing all seams, and for the following construction techniques: Bias-Tape Bound Edges, Sleeves, Double-Turned ¼-Inch Hem, Fastener Application, Basting, Topstitching, Facings and Collars.

1. Fuse the interfacings to both Lab Coat Facings and one Collar piece following manufacturer's instructions. Lay aside.

2. Fold Lab Coat Back (M2) right sides together at center back and stitch on stitching line from neck to X. Press tuck to the right.

3. Topstitch along center back fold from neckline down and across tuck to X (Figure 1).

Figure 1

4. Sew Lab Coat Back (M2) to Lab Coat Fronts (M1) at shoulder seams, matching notches. Press seams open.

5. Construct and baste Collar (M7) to Lab Coat neckline.

6. Construct and stitch Lab Coat Facings (M6) to Lab Coat.

7. Stitch Double-Turned ¼-Inch Hem into sleeve edges.

8. Stitch Sleeves to Lab Coat, matching notches.

9. With right sides together, fold the 2 x 9½-inch rectangle for belt in half lengthwise and stitch (Figure 2).

10. Turn right side out, center seam on back and press, again referring to Figure 2.

Figure 2

11. Mark center of belt and 1 inch on either side of belt center (Figure 3).

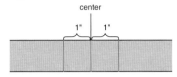

Figure 3

12. Fold belt at center mark, matching the side marks and referring to Figure 4. Pin to hold. Stitch two mini buttons through all thicknesses, again referring to Figure 4.

Figure 4

13. Position belt at positioning marks on back side seams and baste.

14. Make Double-Turned ¼-Inch Hems on top of Pockets (M4, M5). Then, press side and bottom seam allowances toward wrong side.

15. Center and stitch one mini button on top hem of each Pocket.

16. Match circles on Breast Pocket (M5) and squares on Large Pockets (M4) to circles and squares on Lab Coat Fronts (M1) and Topstitch sides and bottoms of all Pockets.

17. Stitch underarm and side seams, matching notches of Lab Coat.

18. Stitch a Double-Turned ¼-Inch Hem in Lab Coat lower edge.

19. Stitch five mini buttons to the right side of the Lab Coat using button placements marked on pattern.

20. Apply three hook-and-loop tape fasteners to the Lab Coat Front.

Scrub Cap

Cutting
Use pattern template M8 (page 44). Transfer all pattern markings to fabric.

From remaining fat quarter:
- Cut two Cap Crown (M8), reversing one.
- Cut one 4 x 14-inch rectangle for Cap band.
- From ½-inch single-fold bias tape:
- Cut one 20-inch length

Assembly
Stitch right sides together using a ¼-inch seam allowance unless otherwise specified. Refer to General Instructions (page 3) for finishing all seams and for Double-Turned ¼-Inch Hem and Single Hem.

1. Make a ½-inch Single Hem on both short ends of the Cap band.

2. Press Cap band in half lengthwise, wrong sides together, and baste raw edges together. Clip close to basting (Figure 5).

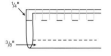

Figure 5

3. Create a casing along the folded edge of the Cap band by stitching ⅜ inch from the fold, again referring to Figure 5.

4. Baste Cap Crown (M8) pieces wrong sides together ¼ inch from the edge.

5. Pin Cap band to Cap Crown at basting line having ends of band meet (Figure 6).

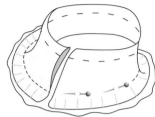

Figure 6

6. Stitch in place and remove basting.

7. Fold bias tape in half lengthwise, wrong sides together, and Topstitch. Thread the bias tape through the Cap band casing using a safety pin or bodkin. Tie knots in the ends of the bias tape.

Scrub Top & Pants
Materials
- 3 coordinating fat quarters (A, B, C)
- 11 inches ¼-inch-wide elastic
- 1 package ½-inch-wide single-fold bias tape
- 1¼ inches ¾-inch-wide fusible hook-and-loop tape
- 2 mini buttons
- Basic sewing supplies and equipment

Cutting
Use pattern templates S1–S6, M3 and M5 (pages 33, 34, 35, 44, 45, 46 and 48). Transfer all pattern markings to fabric.

From fat quarter A:
- Cut two Bodice Upper Fronts (S1), reversing one.
- Cut one Bodice Upper Back (S2).
- Cut two Bodice Lower Fronts (S3).
- Cut one Bodice Lower Back (S4).
- Cut two Sleeves (M3), reversing one.

From fat quarter B:
- Cut two Bodice Upper Fronts (S1), reversing one, for lining.
- Cut one Bodice Upper Back (S2) for lining.

From fat quarter C:
- Cut four Pants Front/Back (S6), reversing two.
- Cut one Large Pocket (M5).
- Cut one Large Pocket Flap (S5).

Assembly
Stitch right sides together using a ¼-inch seam allowance unless otherwise specified. Refer to General Instructions (page 3) for finishing all seams and for the following construction techniques: Bias-Tape Bound Edges, Sleeves, Double-Turned ¼-Inch Hem, Fastener Application and Topstitching.

Scrub Top
1. Stitch Bodice Fronts and Backs together at shoulder seams. Repeat with Lining Bodice Fronts and Backs. Press seams open.

2. With right sides together and matching shoulder seams, stitch the lining to Fronts and Back around neckline. Press lining to inside and baste around armholes.

3. Bind Sleeve cuff edges with bias tape.

4. Stitch Sleeves to Scrub Top, matching notches.

5. Stitch Scrub Top side and underarm seams.

6. Stitch a Double-Turned ¼-Inch Hem on the Bodice Lower Front (S3) center front edges.

7. Stitch Bodice Lower Fronts (S3) to Bodice Lower Back (S4) at side seams, matching notches. Press seams toward back.

8. Stitch upper Scrub Top to lower Scrub Top, matching side seams.

9. Bind Scrub Top hem edge with bias tape.

10. Apply two fusible hook-and-loop tape fasteners to Bodice Upper Fronts along seam line at center front and outer edge.

11. Position and sew two buttons to right side of Upper Scrub Top at seam line referring to Figure 7.

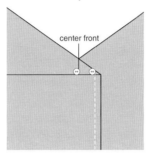

Figure 7

Scrub Pants

1. Stitch Pant Fronts and Backs (S6) together along side seams, matching notches (Figure 8). Press seams to one side and Topstitch in place.

Figure 8

Figure 9

2. Stitch center front Pants seam referring to Figure 9. Press seam to one side and Topstitch in place.

3. Create a waistline elastic casing by pressing on the first fold line to the wrong side. Press again on the second fold line to the wrong side. Stitch close to the first fold line (Figure 10).

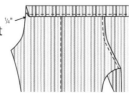

Figure 10

4. Thread elastic through casing, pinning ends of elastic even with back seam. Stitch to secure (Figure 11).

Figure 11

5. Bind pant-leg edges with bias binding.

6. Make Double-Turned ¼-Inch Hems on top of Large Pocket (M5). Then, press side and bottom seam allowances toward wrong side.

7. Match squares on Large Pocket to squares on Scrub Pants, and Topstitch sides and bottoms of all Pockets.

8. Fold Large Pocket Flap (S5) in half, wrong sides together, and stitch short sides together. Turn right side out and press.

9. Match circles on Large Pocket Flap to circles on Scrub Pants and stitch between circles, through Flap and Pants. Press Flap down and Topstitch (Figure 12).

Figure 12

10. Stitch Pant center back seam. Press to one side and Topstitch in place.

11. Sew inner leg seams to complete pant. ❖

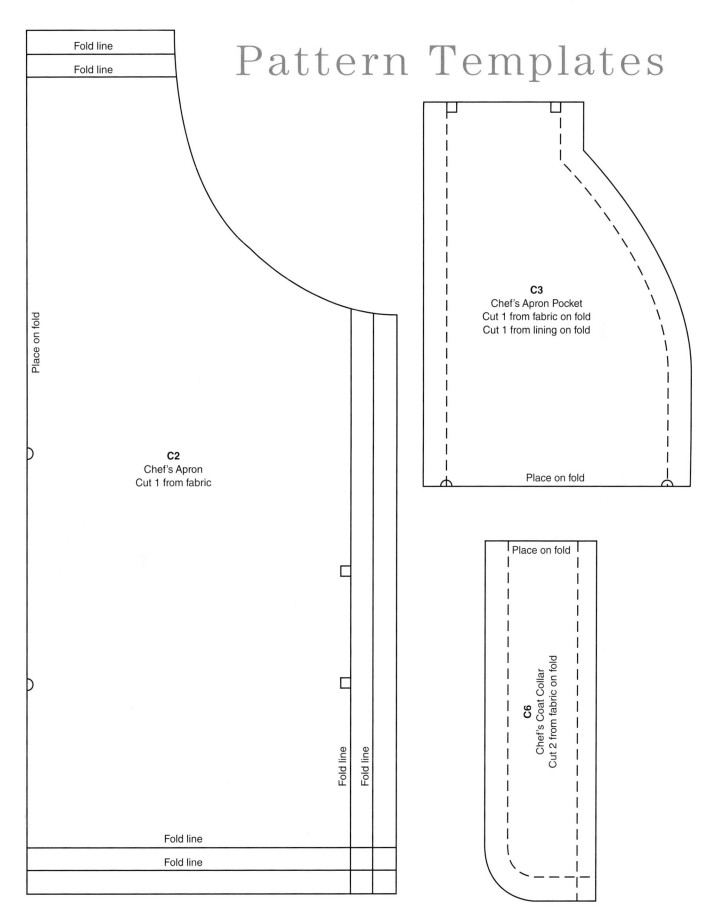

Fold line

Fold line

Pattern Templates

Place on fold

C2
Chef's Apron
Cut 1 from fabric

Fold line

Fold line

Fold line

Fold line

C3
Chef's Apron Pocket
Cut 1 from fabric on fold
Cut 1 from lining on fold

Place on fold

Place on fold

C6
Chef's Coat Collar
Cut 2 from fabric on fold

House of White Birches, Berne, Indiana 46711   Clotilde.com

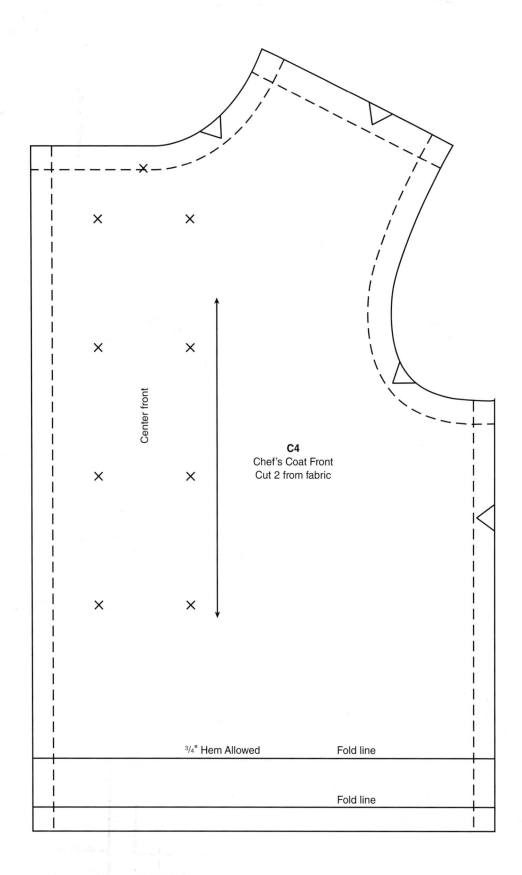

Center front

C4
Chef's Coat Front
Cut 2 from fabric

³/₄" Hem Allowed   Fold line

Fold line

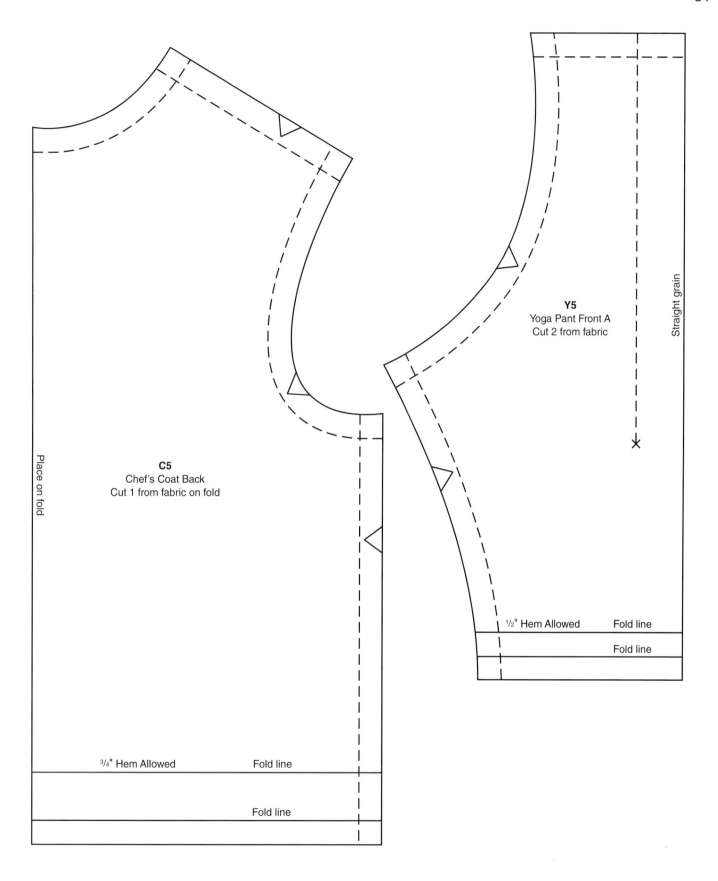

C5
Chef's Coat Back
Cut 1 from fabric on fold

Place on fold

¾" Hem Allowed   Fold line

Fold line

Y5
Yoga Pant Front A
Cut 2 from fabric

Straight grain

½" Hem Allowed   Fold line

Fold line

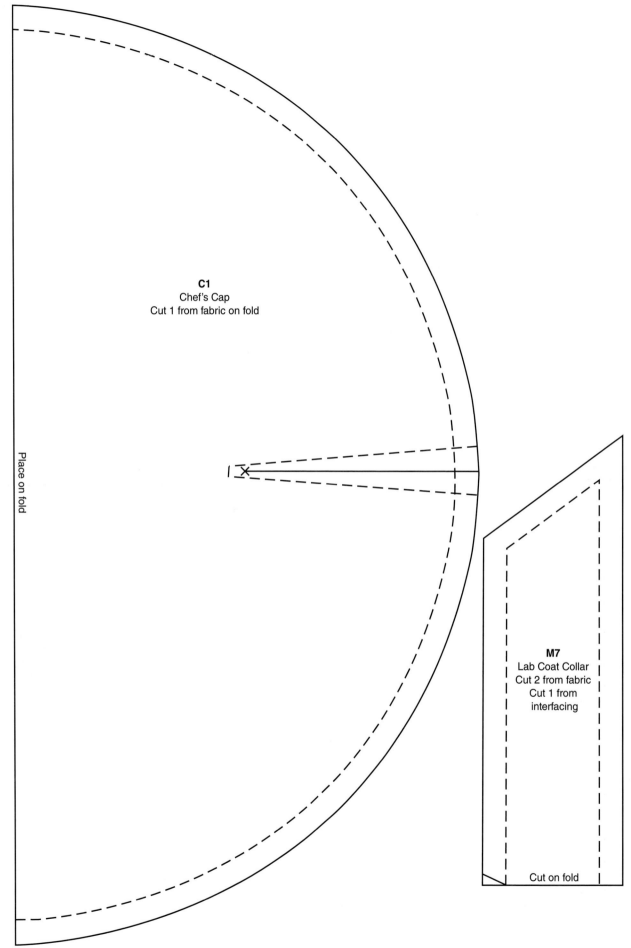

C1
Chef's Cap
Cut 1 from fabric on fold

Place on fold

M7
Lab Coat Collar
Cut 2 from fabric
Cut 1 from
interfacing

Cut on fold

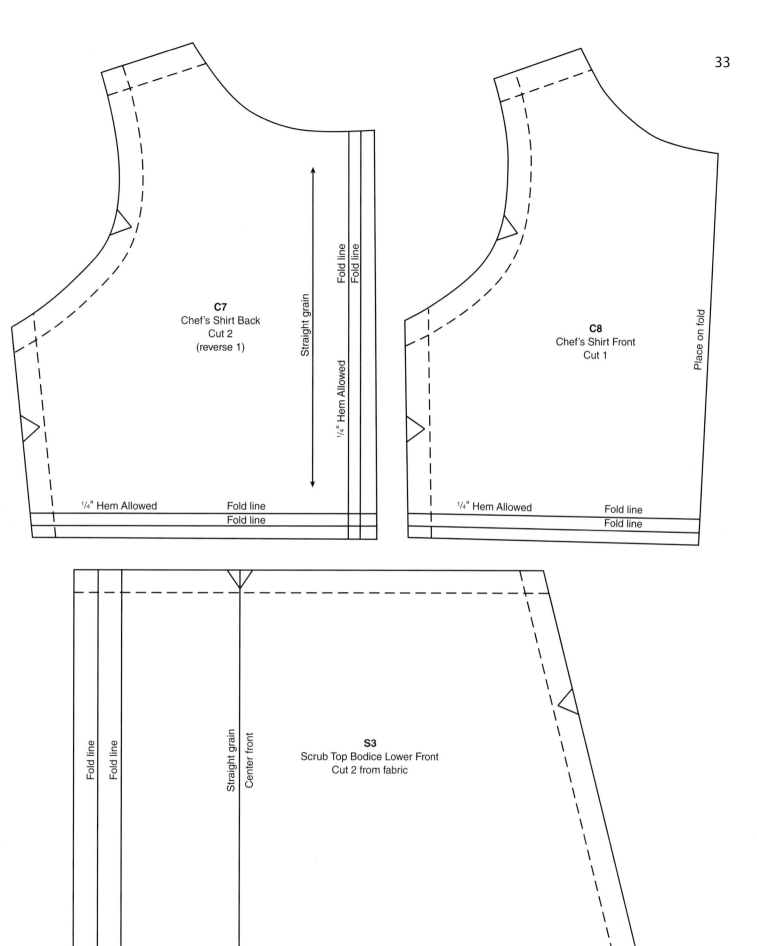

C7
Chef's Shirt Back
Cut 2
(reverse 1)

Straight grain

Fold line

Fold line

1/4" Hem Allowed

1/4" Hem Allowed   Fold line
                         Fold line

C8
Chef's Shirt Front
Cut 1

Place on fold

Fold line

1/4" Hem Allowed   Fold line
                         Fold line

S3
Scrub Top Bodice Lower Front
Cut 2 from fabric

Fold line

Fold line

Straight grain

Center front

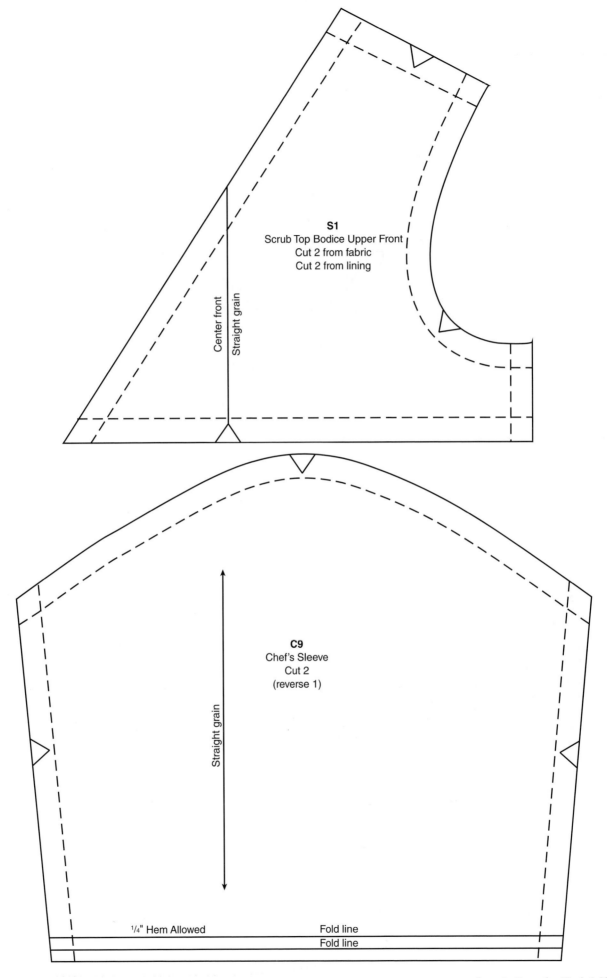

S1
Scrub Top Bodice Upper Front
Cut 2 from fabric
Cut 2 from lining

Center front
Straight grain

C9
Chef's Sleeve
Cut 2
(reverse 1)

Straight grain

¹/₄" Hem Allowed   Fold line
                         Fold line

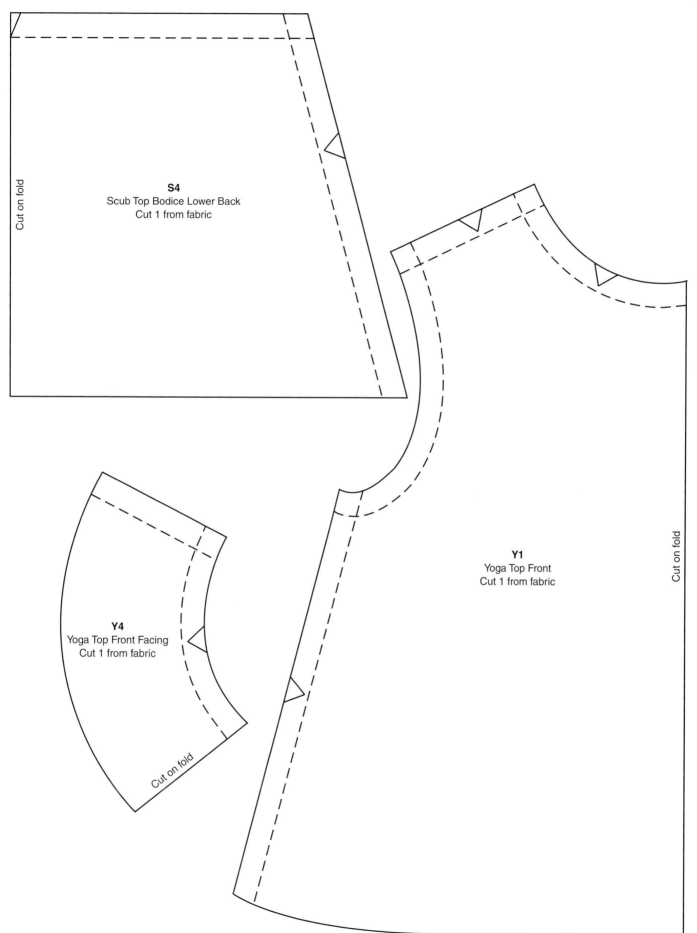

Cut on fold

S4
Scub Top Bodice Lower Back
Cut 1 from fabric

Y1
Yoga Top Front
Cut 1 from fabric

Cut on fold

Y4
Yoga Top Front Facing
Cut 1 from fabric

Cut on fold

House of White Birches, Berne, Indiana 46711   Clotilde.com

36

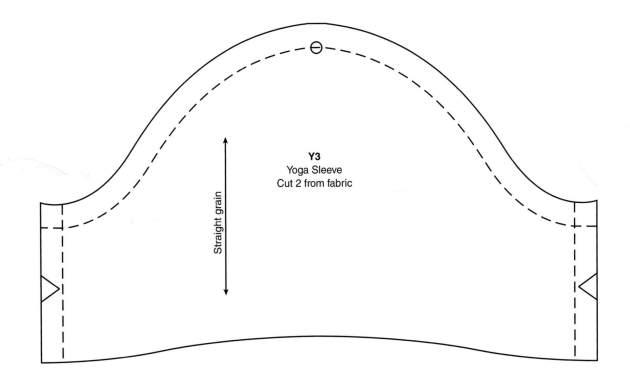

Y3
Yoga Sleeve
Cut 2 from fabric

Straight grain

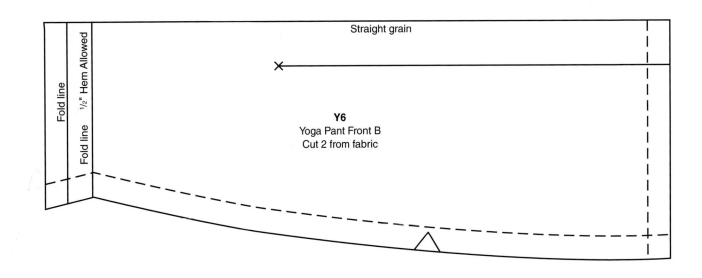

Straight grain

Fold line

Fold line ½" Hem Allowed

Y6
Yoga Pant Front B
Cut 2 from fabric

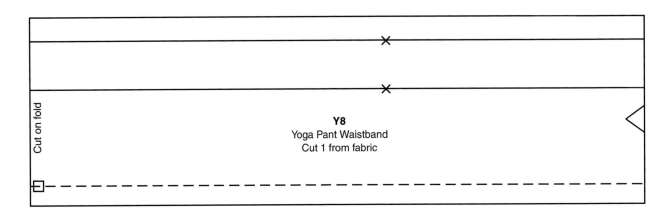

Cut on fold

Y8
Yoga Pant Waistband
Cut 1 from fabric

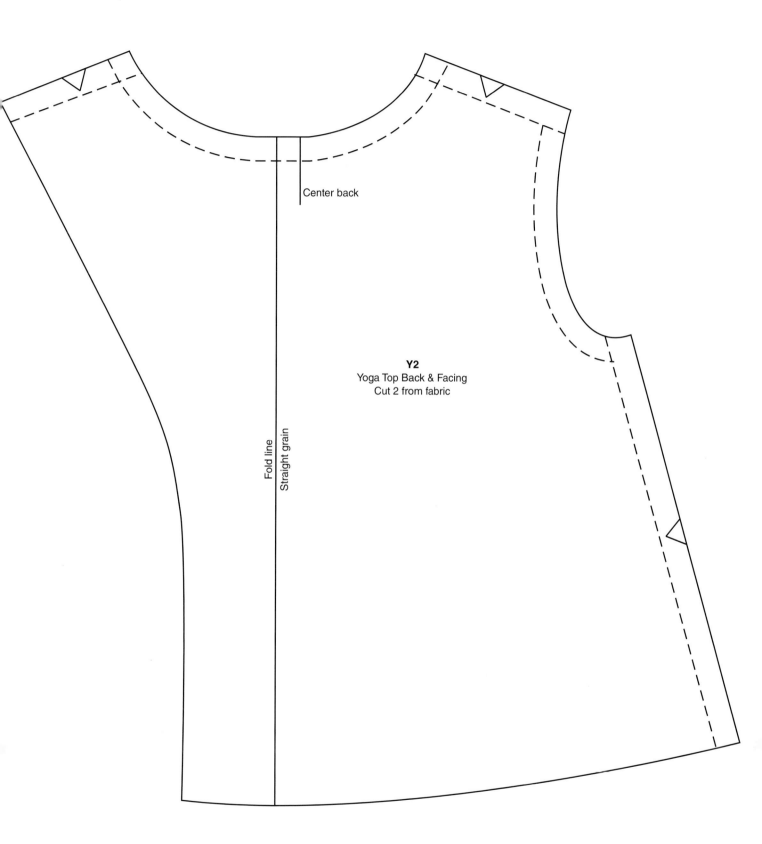

Center back

Y2
Yoga Top Back & Facing
Cut 2 from fabric

Fold line

Straight grain

House of White Birches, Berne, Indiana 46711   Clotilde.com

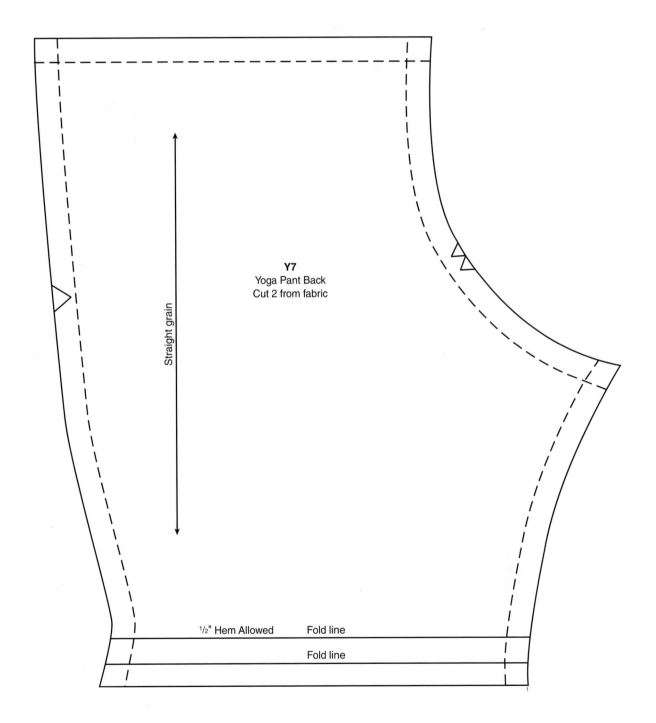

Y7
Yoga Pant Back
Cut 2 from fabric

Straight grain

½" Hem Allowed   Fold line

Fold line

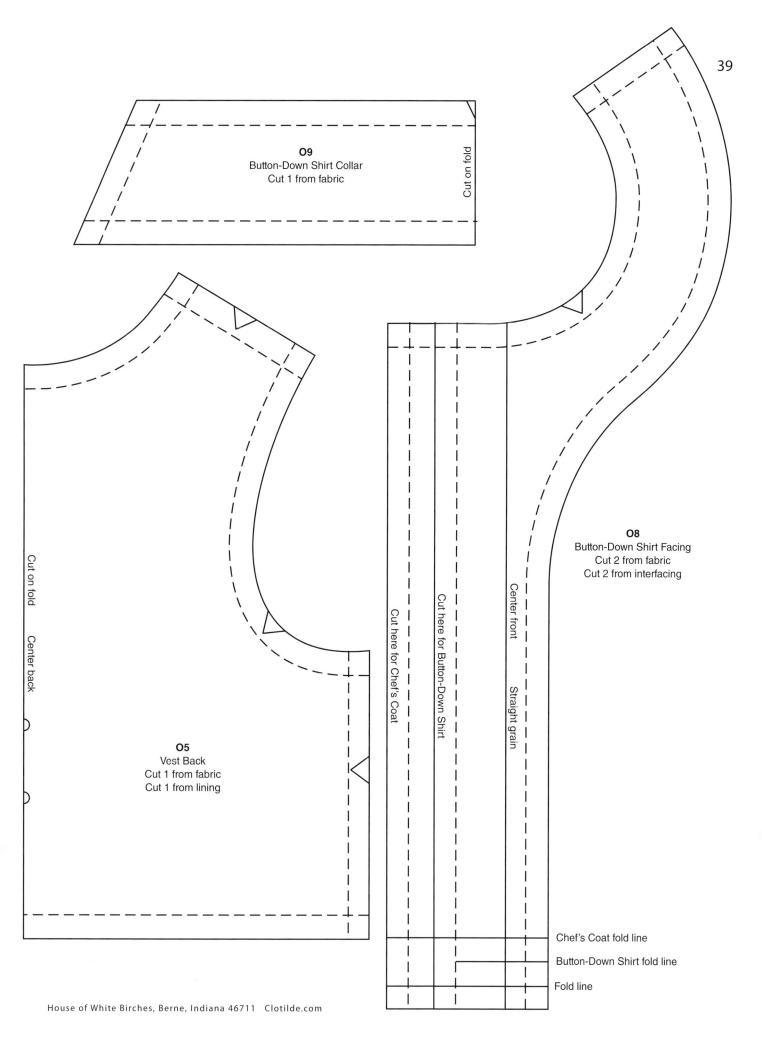

39

O9
Button-Down Shirt Collar
Cut 1 from fabric

Cut on fold

Cut on fold   Center back

O5
Vest Back
Cut 1 from fabric
Cut 1 from lining

Cut here for Chef's Coat

Cut here for Button-Down Shirt

Center front   Straight grain

O8
Button-Down Shirt Facing
Cut 2 from fabric
Cut 2 from interfacing

Chef's Coat fold line

Button-Down Shirt fold line

Fold line

House of White Birches, Berne, Indiana 46711   Clotilde.com

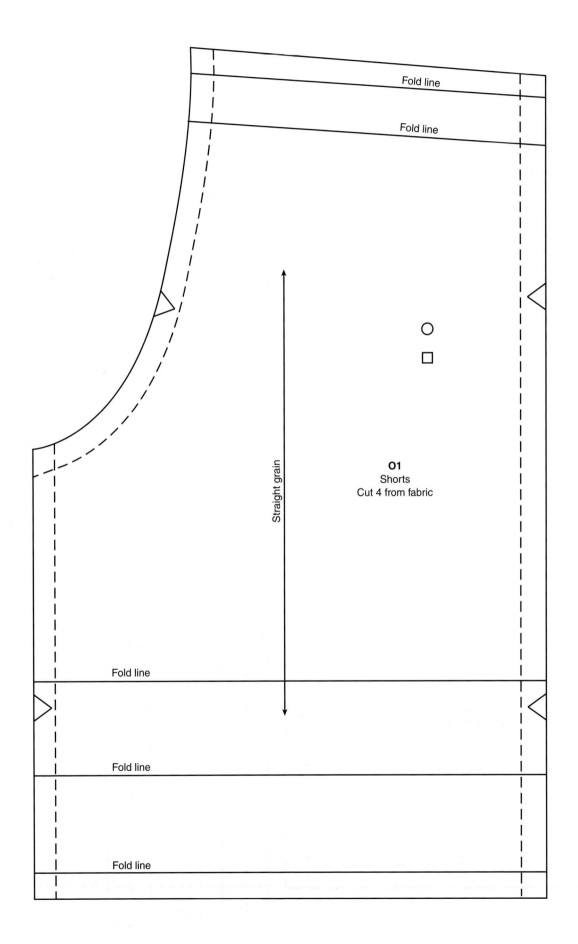

Fold line

Fold line

Straight grain

O1
Shorts
Cut 4 from fabric

Fold line

Fold line

Fold line

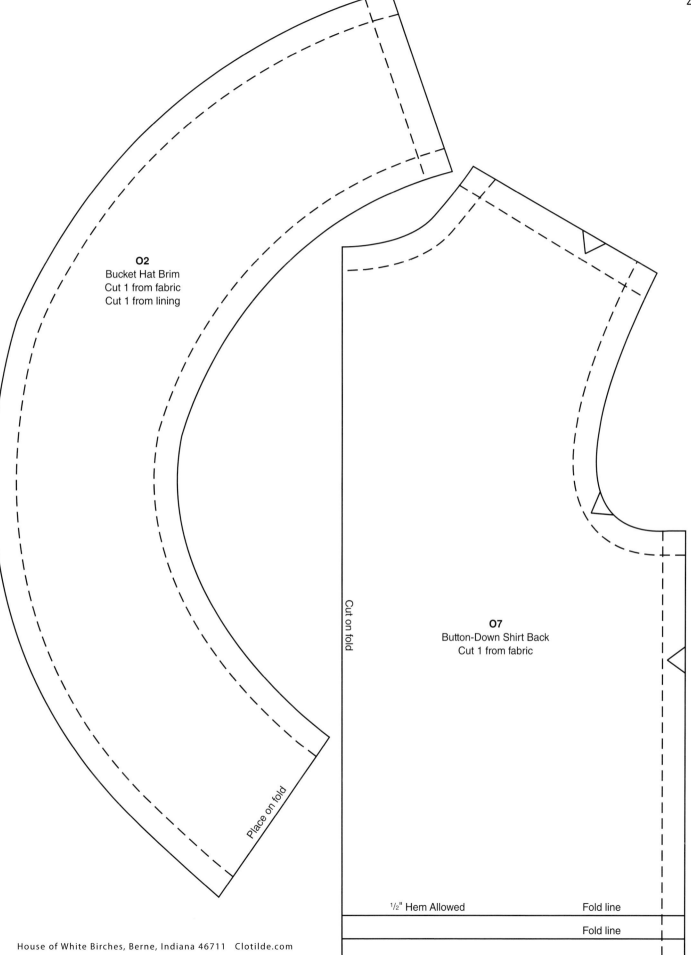

O2
Bucket Hat Brim
Cut 1 from fabric
Cut 1 from lining

Place on fold

Cut on fold

O7
Button-Down Shirt Back
Cut 1 from fabric

½" Hem Allowed

Fold line

Fold line

House of White Birches, Berne, Indiana 46711   Clotilde.com

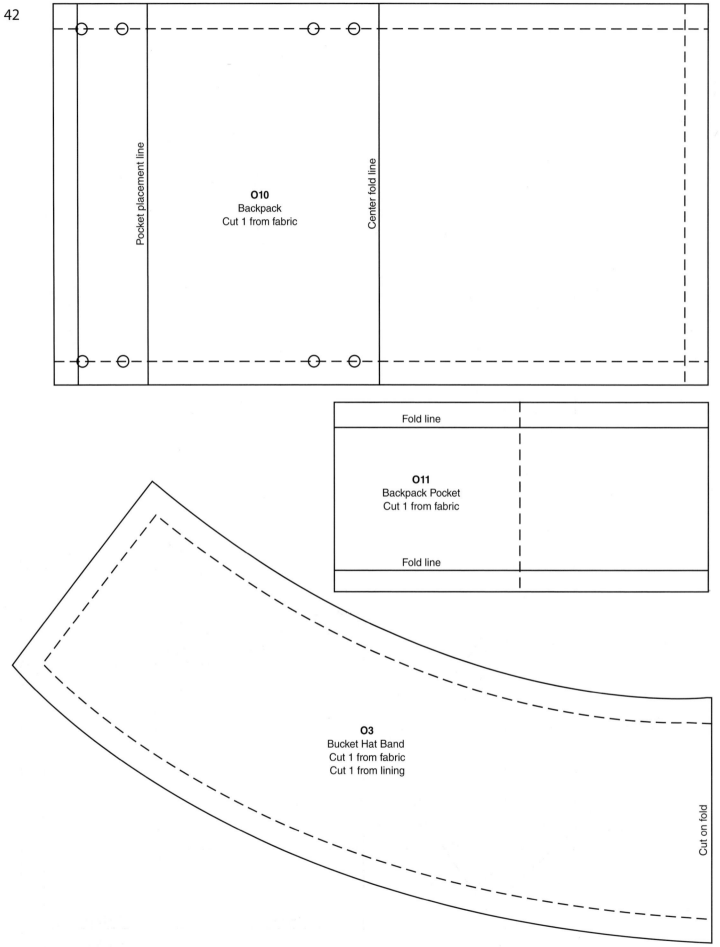

Pocket placement line

O10
Backpack
Cut 1 from fabric

Center fold line

Fold line

O11
Backpack Pocket
Cut 1 from fabric

Fold line

O3
Bucket Hat Band
Cut 1 from fabric
Cut 1 from lining

Cut on fold

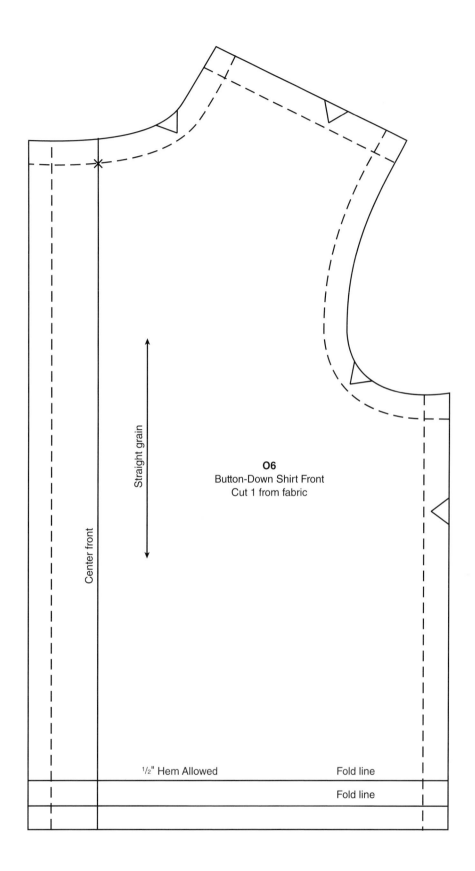

Center front

Straight grain

O6
Button-Down Shirt Front
Cut 1 from fabric

½" Hem Allowed

Fold line

Fold line

House of White Birches, Berne, Indiana 46711   Clotilde.com

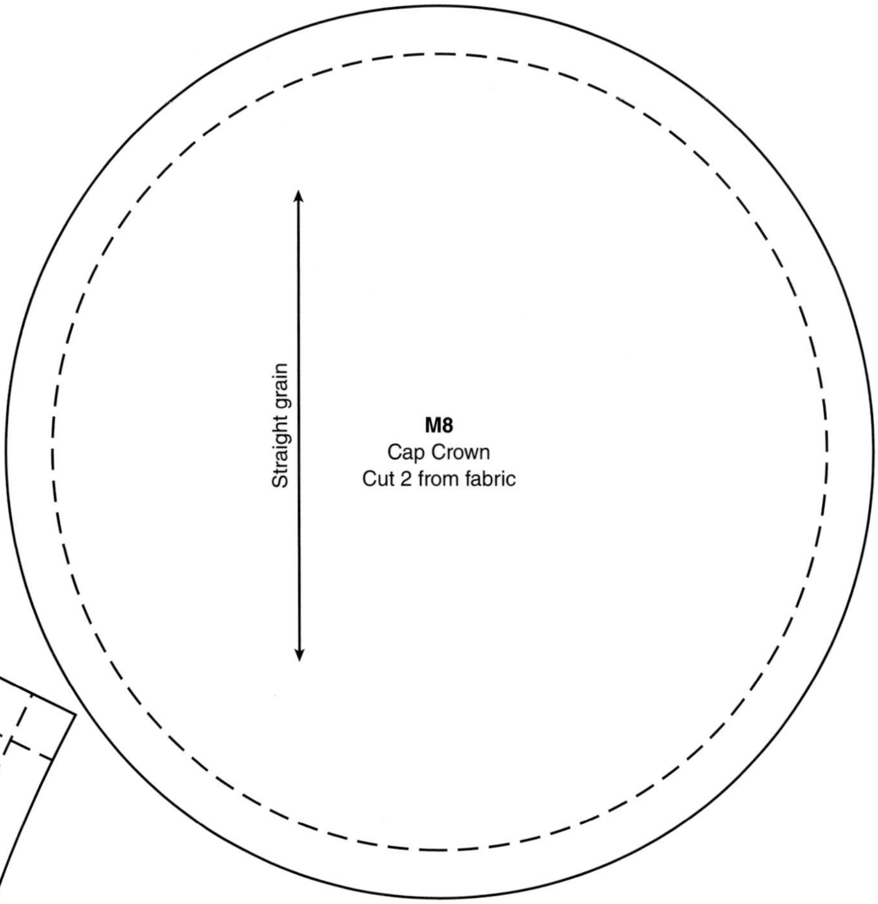

Straight grain

M8
Cap Crown
Cut 2 from fabric

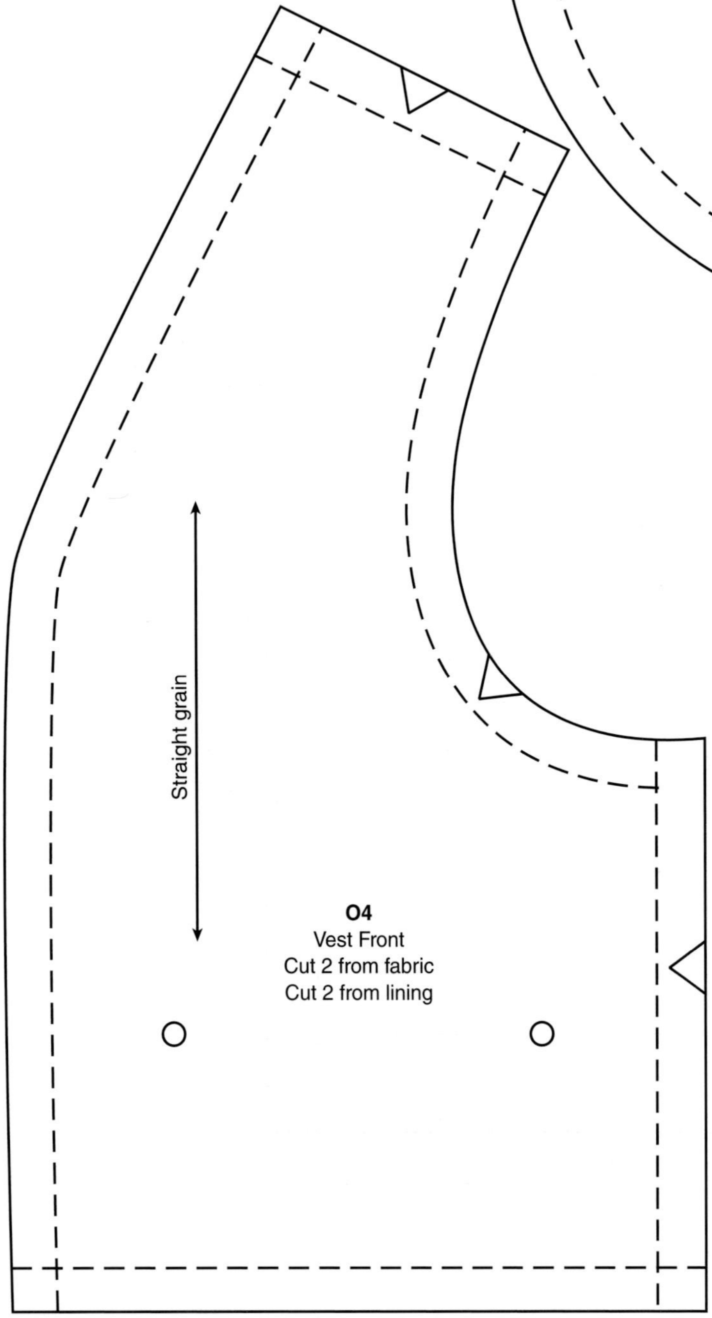

Straight grain

O4
Vest Front
Cut 2 from fabric
Cut 2 from lining

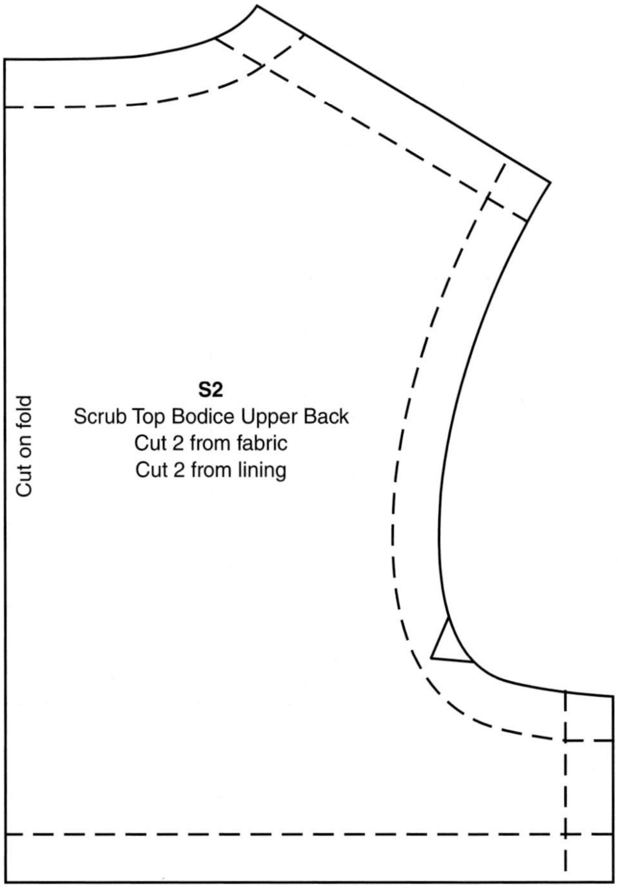

Cut on fold

S2
Scrub Top Bodice Upper Back
Cut 2 from fabric
Cut 2 from lining

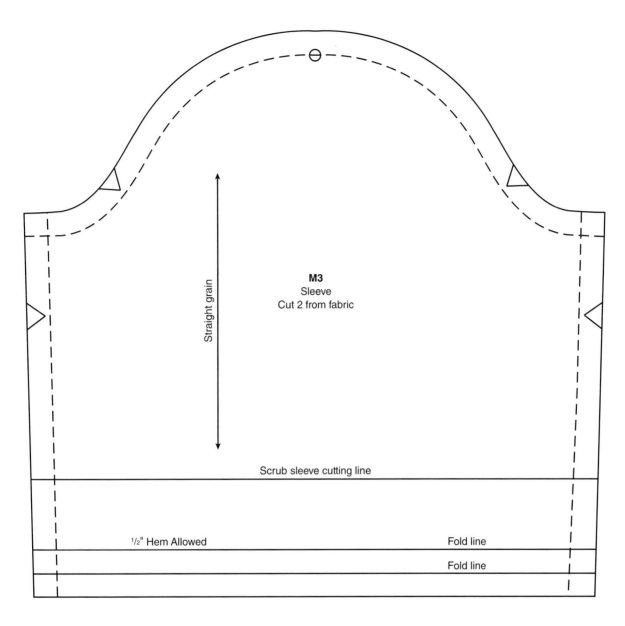

M3
Sleeve
Cut 2 from fabric

Straight grain

Scrub sleeve cutting line

1/2" Hem Allowed

Fold line

Fold line

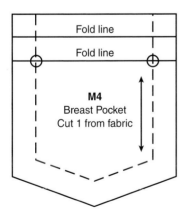

Fold line

Fold line

M4
Breast Pocket
Cut 1 from fabric

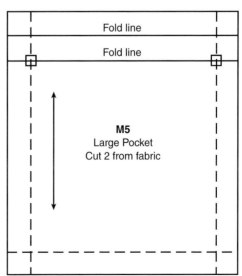

Fold line

Fold line

M5
Large Pocket
Cut 2 from fabric

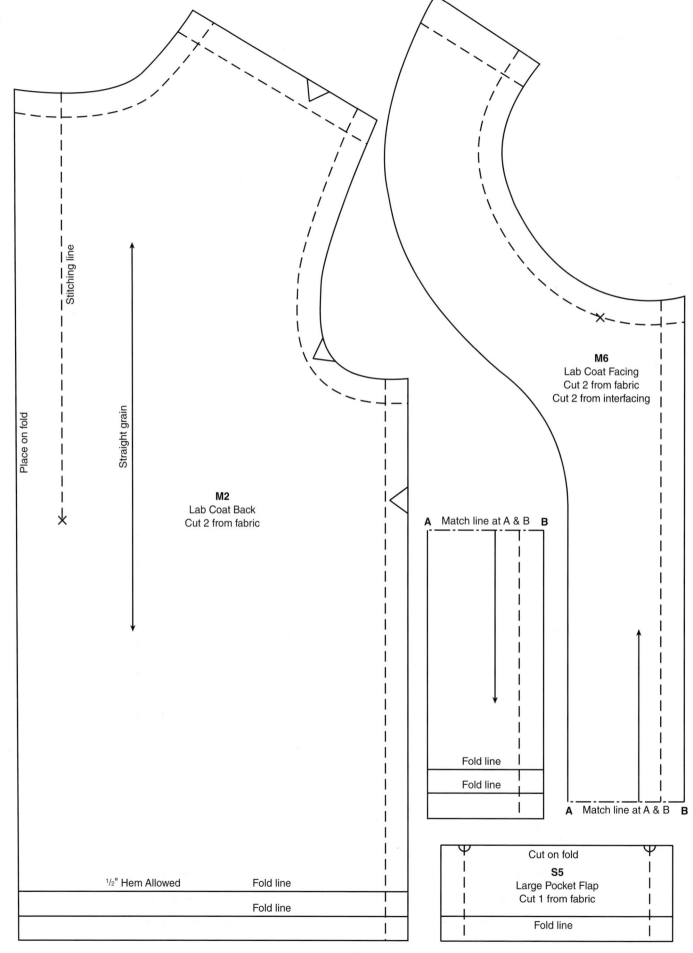

Stitching line

Place on fold

Straight grain

M2
Lab Coat Back
Cut 2 from fabric

M6
Lab Coat Facing
Cut 2 from fabric
Cut 2 from interfacing

A   Match line at A & B   B

A   Match line at A & B   B

½" Hem Allowed   Fold line

Fold line

Fold line

Fold line

Cut on fold

S5
Large Pocket Flap
Cut 1 from fabric

Fold line

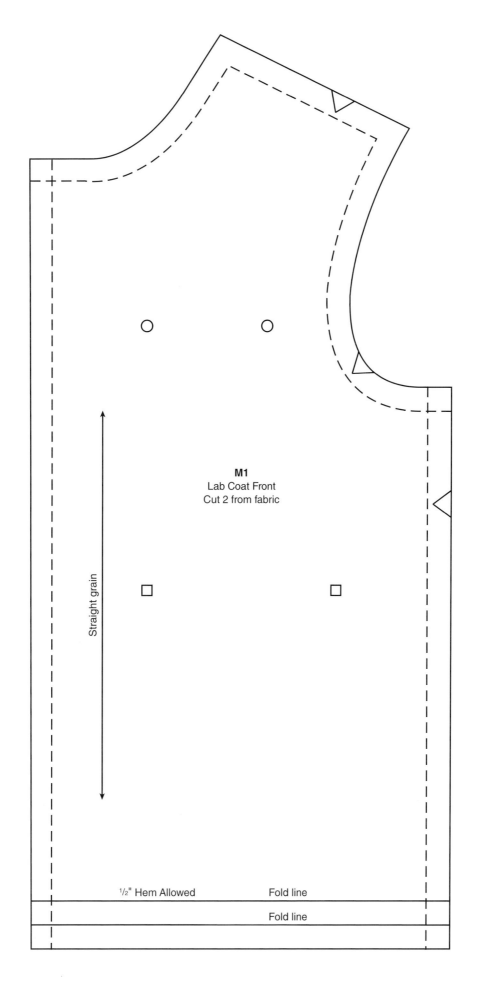

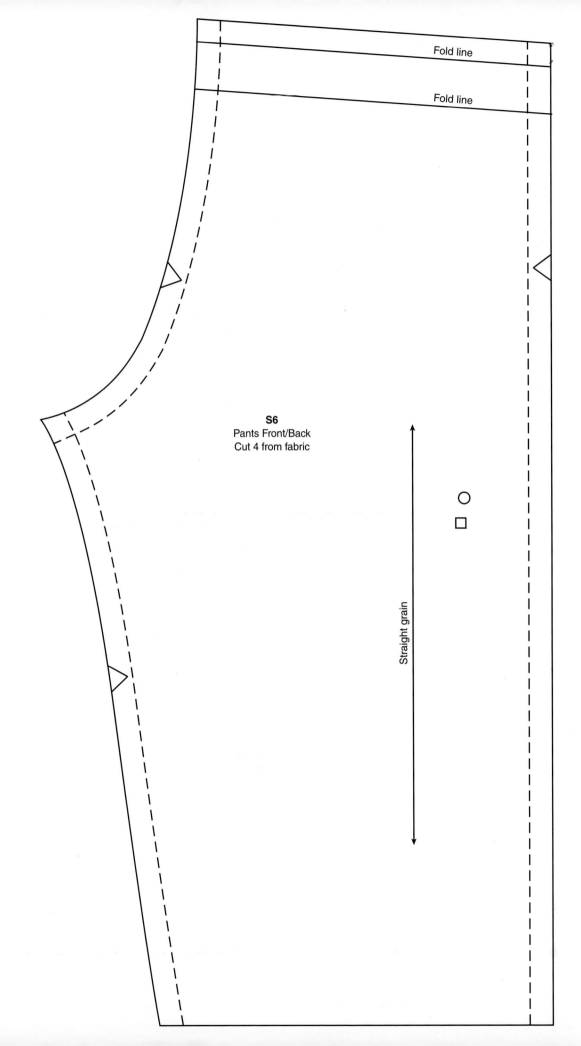

Fold line

Fold line

S6
Pants Front/Back
Cut 4 from fabric

Straight grain